Catch-of-the-Day

Southern Seafood Secrets

(formerly Fripp Island Fare)

Edited and Illustrated by Ginny Lentz and Margaret Terrell
Cover Design by Nancy Ricker Webb

1979

Catch-of-the-Day . . . Southern Seafood Secrets
P.O. Box 1021
Charleston, South Carolina 29402

About our book...

In the winter of 1975, the first edition of our cookbook, then known as *Fripp Island Fare,* came about through the sharing of recipes over a weekly game of bridge.

The four of us, Margaret Terrell, Ginny Lentz Hucks, Jan Reed Kesterson and Bevie Kinder, decided to incorporate these and others in a seafood cookbook. Through the winter months on Fripp Island, we collected and tested recipes, and in April 1975, our first book came off the press.

Fortunately, our recipes proved popular, and that led to a second edition in 1976 with some additions and revisions. Also, by that time our number had been reduced by one, with Bevie Kinder's relocation from Fripp.

For this, our third printing, we have once again revised our book. This is an enriched edition featuring a new title, *Catch-of-the-Day.* To the basic book, we have added some exotic recipes starring unusual local seafoods, plus a new section of complete menus enhanced with historical notes. Again, the passage of time has reduced our little band by one.

We feel our work has now entered its final form, and we sincerely hope that y'all will enjoy these "seafood secrets" as much as all of us have.

Margaret   1978   *Ginny*

Copyright, © 1975 by Fripp Island Fare—Seafood Recipes
    1975   2,000 copies
    1976   3,000 copies

Copyright, © 1978 by Catch-of-the-Day—Southern Seafood Secrets
    1979   5,000 copies
    1979   10,000 copies

International Standard Book Number—0-918544-23-8
Library of Congress Catalog Card Number: 79-66952
All rights reserved

No part of this book may be reproduced or utilized in any form or by any means, electronic or mechanical, including photocopying and recording, or by any information storage and retrieval system, without permission in writing from the publisher.

Printed by Wimmer Brothers Books
P.O. Box 18408
Memphis, TN 38138
"Cookbooks of Distinction"

Southern Seafood Secrets

contents—index

	fish	shrimp	crab	clams	oysters	other ?
appetizers	6	6	10	13	15	16
stews, soups and chowders	18	20	21	25	28	28
main dishes	30	37	56	66	70	75
seafood sauces, etc.			Pages 80-84			
menus			Pages 86-92			

About our sea islands...

History tells us that the inlets and rivers along the Carolina coast once provided safe harbor and an outlet to the sea for the pirates who roamed and plundered the Southern waters and the Caribbean.

'Tis said that these sea islands still hide the buried treasures of Blackbeard and his fellow buccaneers; and on Fripp Island, near Beaufort, South Carolina, there is talk of Captain John Fripp, the privateer, who buried his treasure chests beneath the golden sands and then sailed away never to be heard from again. When the moon rises from the sea and touches the sand with silver, some claim to have seen him returning to retrieve his spoils.

Teeming with deer and raccoon, otter and mink, these coastal islands spring to life at night when the animals come out to feed. In the summer months, the loggerhead turtle returns to the sandy beaches to lay her eggs within a few hundred yards of where she herself was hatched seven years before. Raccoon tiptoe out for midnight oyster suppers or to beg scraps from the passerby, and deer graze by the roadside as you drive up — then turn to dart away into the trees.

These sea islands that provided hunting grounds for the Indians and safe harbor for the buccaneers are today year-round communities for some and provide summer recreation for others. In the inlets and waterways, you can see crabbers with their boats laden with crab traps. Offshore the shrimp boats trawl and the Spanish and king mackerel school in summer, breaking the water in silver streaks.

About the artist...
Nancy Ricker Webb is a nationally recognized watercolor artist who works from her studio in Frogmore, S.C. Her subjects are primarily coastal in origin although she also does illustrations and naturalistic studies. Nancy's paintings of lighthouses along our coast were featured in *South Carolina Wildlife Magazine.*

About the cover...
Nancy has depicted a typical lowcountry shrimp boat heading home with her catch-of-the-day.

appetizers

Saviche (Sa-veé chee)

Combine these in a jar
- 1 lb. raw dolphin, trout or flounder, skinned, deboned, cut in chunks
- ½ c. green peppers, chopped
- 1 c. onions, chopped

Salt well. Cover with lime juice. Turn the jar over to mix ingredients. Refrigerate 2 to 3 days before serving. Serve on picks with Teriyaki Sauce.

Variation: Try raw scallops, crab meat, or red snapper.

Curried Shrimp Dip

Blend until smooth
- 2 - 8 oz. pkg. cream cheese
- ½ pint sour cream

Add and blend well
- 4 T. chutney, minced
- 1½ T. curry powder

Add
- 2 c. diced shrimp

Refrigerate several hours before serving. Garnish with whole shrimp and serve with crackers and chips.

Pickled Shrimp I

Mix together
{
3 lbs. cooked shrimp, peeled
2 c. onion, thinly sliced
1 c. Wesson oil
¼ c. olive oil
¾ c. white vinegar
2½ t. celery seed
2½ T. capers and juice
dash of tabasco
}

Place in glass dish and refrigerate. Make at least one day ahead (preferably three). Stir once a day. Serve with toothpicks.

Pickled Shrimp II

Use small shrimp that have been boiled and peeled. Roll in a little Wesson oil (or similar oil) until shiny. Place the shrimp in a wide-mouthed jar and pour cider vinegar over them until they are barely covered. Drop in several cloves and a clove of garlic. Refrigerate for 24 hours. Remove with slotted spoon and serve.

Variation: Add a bay leaf or a little sugar if a sweeter pickle is desired.

Shrimp Dip

Blend $\Big\{$ 1 lb. cooked shrimp, chopped in chunks
2 - 8 oz. pkg. cream cheese softened with half-and-half or milk

Add to taste $\big\{$ Minced onion and grated onion

Add mayonnaise until you have the desired consistency.

Add dash of $\Big\{$ tabasco
worcestershire sauce
salt and pepper
lemon juice

Serve with chips or crackers.

Party Shrimp Dip

Serves 35

Cook with dill weed in water $\big\{$ 4 lbs. big shrimp

Place drained, peeled shrimp in blender and mince well.

Soften with milk $\big\{$ 4 - 8 oz. pkg. cream cheese

Combine shrimp and cream cheese in large bowl.

Add and mix together $\Big\{$ grated onion
salt
pepper
worcestershire
tabasco
squirt of lemon juice

Serve with crackers or potato chips.

Hot Shrimp or Crab Dip

Melt in a
double boiler
{ 2 sticks garlic cheese
½ stick oleo

Add
{ 1 can shrimp or crab, drained
1 can mushrooms, drained

Serve in chafing dish with melba rounds.

Shrimp Paste

Mix and chill
{ 1 sm. can shrimp (¼ lb. cooked)
1 - 3 oz. pkg. cream cheese
½ c. sour cream
1 pkg. Italian Good Seasons dressing
2 t. lemon juice

Serve with crackers.

Shrimp Salad Mold

Mix together
{ 1½ T. Knox gelatin
1 c. water

Combine with
gelatin mixture
{ 1 can tomato soup
6 oz. cream cheese
½ c. mayonnaise
½ c. celery
½ c. bell pepper
½ c. onion
2 cans shrimp

Pour into mold and chill until firm. Serve with Chicken 'n' Biscuit crackers.

Shrimp and Artichokes Vinaigrette

Make two days ahead and serve cold. Serves 36

Chill thoroughly
{
- 2 - 15 oz. cans artichoke hearts, drained and halved
- 1½ pounds cooked, peeled shrimp
}

Beat together or combine in a blender
{
- 1 egg
- ½ c. vegetable oil
- ½ c. olive oil
- ½ c. wine vinegar
- 2 T. Dijon mustard
- 2 T. chopped chives
- 2 T. minced onions
- ½ t. sugar
- ½ t. salt
- ¼ t. pepper or less
}

Marinate shrimp and artichokes in dressing at least 6 hours. Serve with cocktail forks or picks.

"Cover fresh crab meat with milk before freezing to preserve the flavor and prevent drying."

Island Crab Spread

Combine in baking dish
{
- ¾ c. mayonnaise
- 1 c. crab meat
- 2 t. capers
}

Sprinkle grated cheddar cheese on top.
Bake in 300° oven until bubbly.
Serve on crackers.

Skull Inlet Crab Spread

Mix { 1 - 6½ oz. can crab meat
1 - 8 oz. pkg. cream cheese, softened

Add a little of the juice from the crab meat.

Season to taste with { red pepper
paprika

Pour mixture in a shallow baking dish (greased) and heat in oven until it bubbles. This may be transferred to a chafing dish and served with crackers as an appetizer.

Variation: This recipe may be used as a main dish.

Hot Crab Cocktail Spread

Combine { 1 - 8 oz. pkg. cream cheese
1 T. milk
2 t. worcestershire

Add { 1 - 6½ oz. can crab meat, or
equivalent amount fresh crab
2 T. green onion, chopped

Turn into shallow baking dish or 8 inch pie pan. Top with 2 T. slivered almonds. Bake at 350° for 15 minutes.

Serve on warming tray with assorted crackers. Ritz-type crackers seem best.

 # Marinated Crab Claws

Hold crab claw by fixed pincer, taking moveable pincer in other hand. Bend the moveable portion back and forth until it separates and can be pulled out of the main part with the meat intact. It may be necessary to crack the crab claw to make it come out whole.

Place claws in a large jar and cover with Italian dressing. Place in refrigerator overnight.

Arrange the claws around a large dish with a bowl of cocktail sauce (p. 80) in the center.

Crab-Swiss Bites

Makes 36

Combine and mix well
{
- 1 - 6½ oz. can crab meat, drained and flaked
- 1 T. green onion, chopped
- 4 oz. Swiss cheese, shredded
- ½ c. mayonnaise
- 1 t. lemon juice
- ¼ t. curry powder

Take 1 package of a dozen flaky refrigerator rolls and separate each one into three layers. Place on an ungreased baking sheet and spoon on crab mixture. Top each with a few slices of water chestnut. Bake at 400° for 10-12 minutes or until golden brown.

Clams In Garlic Butter

Steam clams and remove from shells. Blend with melted garlic butter and parsley. These may be served at a party in a chafing dish, or on the half-shell with toast as an hors d'oeuvre.

Clam Dip

Mix together
- ½ lb. of cream cheese
- ½ t. salt
- 1 can minced clams, drained

After ingredients have been mixed together, moisten with beer until it is the proper dip consistency.

Spicy Clam Dip

"Make earlier in the day so the flavor has a chance to penetrate."

Blend thoroughly
- 1 can minced clams, drained
- 2 - 3 oz. pkgs. cream cheese with chives
- 3 t. worcestershire
- 1 T. lemon juice
- 2 T. mayonnaise
- 10 drops tabasco

Clam Fondue

"Serves a small crowd "

Mix together
{
- 2 - 8 oz. pkgs. softened cream cheese
- 2 cans clams, minced and drained (reserving juice)
- 1 - 8 oz. container sour cream
- ½ t. lemon juice
- 1 t. grated onion
- 1 T. sherry
- 1 t. worcestershire
- salt to taste

Add ½ of reserved clam juice. Refrigerate until ready to serve; then heat thoroughly. Add rest of clam juice if needed for proper consistency.

Serve in chafing dish with corn chips or toast squares.

Stuffed Clams

Place 18 large well-scrubbed clams in a kettle with enough water to cover the bottom. Cover kettle with a lid and steam until shells open. Remove the meat from the shells, discarding the tough necks. Finely mince the clams.

Mix with
{
- 2 T. chives, minced
- 2 T. onion, finely chopped
- 3 T. mushrooms, minced and sauteed 1 minute in butter
- 1 t. parsley, minced
- 2 T. fine bread crumbs

Stir in 1 t. sherry and enough white wine to moisten the mixture. Heap onto half shell and sprinkle with buttered bread crumbs. Bake at 350° for 15 minutes.

Variation: Sprinkle top with Parmesan cheese.

Oyster Delight

Wrap whole raw oysters in bacon. Secure with a toothpick. Broil until crisp all around.

Oyster Dip

Cook until soft { ½ stick butter, melted
1 green onion with tops, chopped
2 T. green pepper, chopped

Add 2 T. flour and stir. Then add a little milk and stir until smooth. This will be thick.

Add { 1 sm. can mushrooms and juice
salt, black and red pepper to taste
paprika for color
worcestershire to taste
½ wedge Cracker Barrel mellow cheese

Stir until cheese is melted and ingredients are well-blended.

Drain 1 pt. oysters, reserving juice. Slowly add juice to the mixture until it is a good consistency. Cut oysters in two or three pieces and add to mixture. Serve from chafing dish with melba rounds or in pastry shells.

Variation: Add more cheese to make this recipe a main dish.

Periwinkles or "Estuarine Escargots"

Periwinkles are the small black snails that abound in the marshes and creek grasses.

Scrub shells until clean. Then cover with "a knuckle's length" of salted water. Boil for 20-25 minutes. Serve with toothpicks and dill or garlic butter.

> Today the natural beauty of the Sea Islands and estuaries of the Southern coast attract tourists and retirees, who find there a life rich in physical abundance and spiritual pleasures.

Sauteed Scallops

"This recipe will serve two as a main dish, or four as an hors d'oeurve. For a uniquely delicious taste treat, this is a must to try!"

Serves 2-4

Saute until liquid evaporates:
- 1 lb. scallops, washed and cut in bite-size pieces
- ¼ stick butter
- salt and pepper
- juice of ½ large lemon or whole small one

Then combine:
- ½ c. sherry
- 1 t. sugar

Pour over scallops and cook until most of the sherry has cooked away.

stews, soups and chowders

Catch-of-the-day Bouillabaise

Skin all fish, shrimp and lobster. Place all peelings and skins in large pot filled with water. Add salt, pepper, seafood seasoning, thyme and rosemary. Simmer 3 to 4 hours, reducing your liquid to a tasty fish stock.

Heat in shallow pan (do not overcook)
- filleted fish chunks
- shrimp
- lobster

Add 1 oz. Cognac. Ignite and immediately put out the fire by covering with lid.

Strain stock, add to clear broth and cook 'til tender
- diced carrots
- diced celery
- diced onions
- diced potatoes

Add and bring to boil
- fish
- shrimp
- lobster

Transfer to serving bowl; garnish with chopped parsley.

Variations: If available, add shucked oysters and clams. For a very festive appearance, leave clams in their shells but be sure to scrub them first.

Beaufort Fish Chowder

Cover with cold water
in large pot
{
3 or 4 whole fish (cleaned, scaled beheaded)
2 bay leaves
1 large onion, sliced
1 carrot, sliced
1 stalk celery with leaves, cut up
peppercorns
tabasco
salt
}

Bring to a boil. Simmer until meat falls from bones. Cool; then strain broth and set aside.

Remove meat from bones, taking care to find all the little bones. Set fish aside.

Fry out
{
2 inch cubes of fatback
(salt pork)
}

Use grease to
lightly saute
{
2 onions, chopped
2 large stalks celery, finely chopped
}

Add to broth along with
{ 2 large potatoes, finely diced }

Boil until potatoes are done.

Add and simmer 10 min.
{
fish
2 cans evaporated milk
1 can water
}

Correct seasonings: black pepper, BeauMonde, MSG, tabasco, or your own favorite seafood seasoning.

Variations: This recipe can be used with bass, trout, and whiting. It is basic and you may add your own touches of seasoning, vegetables, etc. . and make it thicker or thinner according to personal preference.

Fish Stew

Cut ¼ lb. bacon in small pieces and fry until crisp. Remove from pan and drain. Saute 1 large onion (chopped) in bacon drippings.

Add and cook 30-45 minutes
{
1 #2 can tomatoes
1 can tomato soup or sauce
1 can water
1 t. sugar
3 T. worcestershire
½ bottle catsup
salt
red pepper or hot sauce
}

Add raw fish fillets during the last 15 minutes of cooking time. (Frozen flounder fillets are good if fresh fish fillets are not available.)

Top with bacon bits and serve in soup bowls over rice.

Variation: Serve stew in individual bowls without rice as an appetizer.

Shrimp Soup

"May be frozen for later use."

Simmer 20 minutes
{
2 cans shrimp bisque
1 - 13 oz. can evaporated milk
1 can pepperpot soup
1 can chicken gumbo soup
2 T. butter
1 - 6½ oz. can crab meat
1 can bisque of tomato
½ cup sherry
}

Stir occasionally while simmering. Serve with a fruit salad and crackers. Leftover soup may be frozen for later use.

Blue Channel Crab Stew

Serves 5

Rinse in cold water and remove any shell pieces
- 2 - 6½ oz. cans Harris Atlantic Claw Crab Meat

Saute until transparent
- 2 T. butter
- 2 T. onion, diced

Add to onion and simmer for five minutes before serving. (Do not boil)
- crab meat
- 3 c. milk
- 13 oz. evaporated milk
- 1 chicken bouillon cube
- salt and pepper

Consumer's Crab Talk

"Crab meat is a seasonless seafood available in several forms."

FRESH — unprocessed, carefully picked and iced; good for about one week

PASTEURIZED — carefully picked, minimally cooked, refrigerated; good for several months if NOT opened

STERILIZED — carefully picked, pressure cooked 'til germ free; good for several years without refrigeration

FROZEN — carefully picked and fast frozen in air-tight containers or freezing bags

"Cover crab meat with milk before freezing. This prevents freezer burn."

"Crab meat varies in taste, color, size and age..."

BACKFIN LUMP — two large back swimmer muscles inside the body cavity of every crab

FLAKY WHITE — body crab meat, smaller than lump but just as tasty

CLAW MEAT — while darker, considered by many to be the tastiest

SOFT SHELL — a recently molted crab, available to consumers year-round (frozen), caught only in the summer months

Fripp Island Crab Stew

Saute
: 2 T. butter
: ½ onion, chopped

Add
: 1 t. parsley
: ¾ t. garlic salt
: juice from drained crab meat

Thicken with 1 T. flour. Slowly add ½ pint of heavy cream and stir until thick.

Then add
: ½ pint milk
: 2 potatoes, cooked & diced
: 1 lb. lump crab meat, or 2 cans
: worcestershire sauce
: cayenne pepper
: salt and pepper

Let simmer. Do not allow to boil. Just before serving add ⅓ to ½ c. sherry.

Cathy's Crab Soup

Combine and heat
: 1 can green pea soup
: 1 can tomato soup
: 1 soup can water
: 1 T. curry powder
: sherry to taste
: 10 to 12 oz. crab meat

Aunt Anna's She-Crab Soup

10 one cup servings

Saute until soft, not brown.	{ 1 medium onion, chopped ½ stick butter dash of nutmeg dash of MSG
Add and heat	{ 1 lb. white crab meat
In double boiler, heat	{ 7½ c. milk 1 pt. half & half
Add	{ crab meat mixture another ½ stick butter
Season with	{ worcestershire salt & pepper

Stir cornstarch (1 to 5 t.) depending on desired thickness into ½ c. milk. Add to soup to thicken.

Add ¼ c. chopped crab roe. If soup is too thick, thin with ¼ c. sherry wine.

Serve hot in warm bowls with sherry to taste. Float the wine on top of the soup.

"Substitute crumbled egg yolks for crab roe in She Crab Soup recipes."

"Always throw back females with egg sack *outside* under their aprons. The golden roe, used in She-Crab soups, can only be found *inside* the female."

She-Crab Soup (Condensed Version)

see page 93

Tidalholm Seafood Chowder

"May be frozen for later use."

Saute in ½ stick of butter about 3-4 minutes
{ ¼ c. diced oysters and liquid
1 c. small peeled raw shrimp

Add and turn heat LOW
{ 1 qt. milk

Add and cook VERY SLOWLY for 10 minutes. Stir often.
{ ½ c. crab meat
1 small can water chestnuts, thinly sliced, and the liquid
1 can whole kernel corn and the liquid
1 c. cooked white potatoes, diced and liquid
1½ c. cooked fish, diced (can be leftover, baked fish)
salt and pepper to taste
parsley (optional)

Then add 1 pint of half-and-half and heat another minute VERY CAREFULLY stirring. (Too much heat will cause the half-and-half to separate). If freezing is desired, omit potatoes until serving time.

Variations: Add or delete seafoods as available.
   Thicken this recipe and serve over a basic omelet, page 62.

"When shucking oysters or clams, always reserve the liquor to be added to chowders."

Bob's "Damn Good Clam Chowder"

Stew one chicken* (or use 4 backs, 4 wings and any other parts you have) in 2 gals. of water until meat is done. Remove chicken from broth.

Add to broth and cook until done	{ 6 carrots, chopped 1½ c. celery, chopped 8 potatoes, chopped
Saute in fry pan	{ 1 stick of butter 5 onions, chopped
Add to fry pan	{ 24 med. size clams, chopped (Reserving juice)

Cook for 3 to 5 minutes. Add ½ c. flour to 1½ c. water to make flour paste. Pour into onion and clam mixture, stirring constantly. Simmer until thickened. Stir in reserved clam juice.

When clam juice is blended pour the onion and clam mixture into broth with vegetables, stirring constantly.

Add	{ 1 c. milk salt and pepper to taste ¼ t. Accent

Bring to slow boil, turn down and simmer for 30 minutes or longer.

*Variation: Cooked, deboned chicken may be added if desired.

"Clams can be chopped quickly in a blender or food processor."

Clif's Clam Chowder

Grind in food chopper ⎰ 1 qt. clams
⎱ 8 medium potatoes
   8 medium onions

Place this in heavy pot and cover with water. Cook over low heat until potatoes are soft.

Add to the above ⎰ 4 T. bacon drippings
   2 cans tomatoes
   ½ bottle ketchup
   4 T. worcestershire
   1 t. hot pepper sauce
⎱ salt and pepper to taste

Add enough water to make 1 gallon.

Simmer for 1 hour, stirring so that it won't stick.

"Shellfish" aren't really fish. They are salt or fresh water invertebrate animals with one or more shells. Mollusks (oysters, clams and scallops) and crustaceans (shrimp, crab, lobster, and crayfish) are examples."

Ginny's Clam Chowder

"May be frozen for later use."

Serves 8-10

Saute in deep
kettle until golden-brown
{
4 slices bacon, chopped
2 med. onions, chopped
2 stalks celery, chopped
2 carrots, chopped
1 green pepper, chopped

Add and briefly
saute
{
1 clove garlic, minced
1 t. paprika

Add and stir
{
1 sachet bag or
 ¼ t. thyme
 ¼ t. rosemary
 1 bay leaf

Add
{
3 doz. clams (about 1 qt.)
 minced, reserving liquor
3 med. potatoes, cubed
1 c. tomatoes, chopped (opt.)
½ c. tomato sauce or puree (opt.)

Cover with just enough water or clam broth to cook the clams and potatoes. Simmer for 30 minutes.

Add and stir well
{
3 c. clam liquor, strained through 2
 layers of cheesecloth
1 qt. milk
1 t. salt
¼-½ t. freshly ground pepper

Thicken with paste of 3 T. flour and 3 T. butter.

Cover and simmer 1 hour stirring occasionally. Before serving add 2 T. fresh parsley and 2 T. butter.

Serve piping hot with crackers, spoonbread, or cornsticks. This can be frozen for future use, but omit potatoes until serving time.

Oyster Stew or Chowder

6 servings

Cook 3 minutes until oysters begin to curl.	1 pint oysters, fresh or thawed and liquor ½ stick butter, melted
Add. Heat thoroughly by simmering but do NOT boil.	1 quart milk or half-and-half 1½ t. salt or less ⅛ t. pepper **- For Chowder -** sauteed chopped onion (opt.) sauteed chopped celery (opt.) cooked diced white potatoes (opt.) undrained whole kernel corn (opt.)
Garnish with	paprika sprigs of parsley
Serve at once with	corn sticks oysterettes, etc.

Coquina Chowder

For the uninitiated, coquinas are the tiny clam-like creatures in rainbow colors that are found in the surf as the waves hit the sand. The best way to catch these is with a rice colander.

Bring to a brisk boil in a large pot	4 or 5 qts. coquinas cold water to just beneath top layer of shells

Cover, and turn heat down. Simmer for 5 minutes. Coquinas will open and their delicate, briny juice will blend in with pot water. Strain the liquid (about 1 qt.) into another pot.

Add and simmer until tender	2-2½ c. Irish potatoes, finely diced
Then add	2-2½ c. heavy cream

Stir 2-3 minutes and serve. Garnish with paprika or parsley. This will probably not need any salt. Season mildly so as not to disturb the delicate flavor.

main dishes

FISH FACTS

— Fish are easier to cook than hamburgers!
— Almost any kind of fish can be broiled or fried.
— Fatty fish contain more than 5% fat and can also be baked, grilled or smoked. (Examples: mackerel, pompano, tuna, mullet, and eel)
— Lean fish contain less than 5% fat and have firmer flesh. Good poached, steamed, in chowders, or baked—basting with butter or oil to prevent drying. (Examples: flounder, trout, red snapper, grouper and bass)

Baked Stuffed Fish

"Particularly good with Spanish mackerel, cobia, or sheepshead."

Saute until soft
{ ⅓ c. butter, melted
½ c. onion, chopped
¾ c. celery, chopped
¼ c. bell pepper, chopped

Add and cook 5 min. over low heat
{ 1 c. crab meat
1 c. small or diced shrimp
1 c. stuffing mix or cracker crumbs
1 beaten egg

This makes enough stuffing for a 2½ to 3 lb. fish.

Stuff fish. Back bone is usually removed to make room for the stuffing. Bake in dish greased with lemon butter at 325° to 350° for 45 minutes to an hour. Baste about every 10 minutes with melted lemon-butter. Add strips of bacon to fish for last 15 minutes, if desired.

Lemon-butter may also be seasoned with parsley flakes, celery salt and oregano. See page 81.

Trout Amandine

Serves 4

Mix { 1 stick butter, melted
1 c. slivered almonds

Place over low heat. Meanwhile . . .

Take 8-10 trout fillets (depending on how hungry you are) and coat with flour and salt and pepper. Cook in butter until just done.

Place fish in one layer in baking dish and pour butter and almonds over them. Squeeze the juice of one lemon on top and bake 5-10 minutes at 350°.

Variation: Use flounder in place of trout.

"Overcooking spoils the flavor and texture of fish; cook ONLY 'til flesh is flaky."

Fillets of Trout in Sour Cream

Place trout fillets in baking dish and sprinkle with 1 oz. dry vermouth.

Combine { 1 c. sour cream
¼ c. Parmesan cheese
1 T. lemon juice
1 T. onion, grated
½ t. salt

Spread mixture over the fillets. Sprinkle with paprika and bake at 350° for 25-30 minutes. Garnish with parsley and lemon and serve.

Variation: *This recipe can be used with <u>kingfish steaks as well as other fish</u>. Add a dash of hot pepper sauce to spice up the flavor and sprinkle with paprika.*

Rule of Thumb for cooking fish—For every knuckle's length of thickness (side to side) allow about 10 minutes of cooking time at 450°.

Bonito (Little Tunny)

Use clean, skinless, boneless fillets cut into chunks.

Saute 1 chopped onion until clear. Add the fish and 2 cloves of minced garlic and simmer a little longer.

Add
- 1 c. canned, stewed tomatoes
- 1 c. diced potatoes
- 1 bay leaf
- dash of cayenne pepper
- a few strips of pimiento

Cover and simmer this for 1 hour. Season with salt and pepper.

Bluefish — Grilled or Baked

Place dressed bluefish on a large piece of foil.

Sprinkle inside and out with
- paprika
- lemon pepper
- oregano
- salt and pepper
- Parmesan cheese (opt.)
- parsley (opt.)

Dab with butter and lemon slices. Seal foil tightly and grill or bake until the fish is flaky.

"When freezing raw bluefish, place pieces in container and cover with water."

King or Spanish Mackerel

Broil mackerel previously brushed with butter, salt and pepper.

Halfway through cooking, pour on the following mustard sauce and finish broiling.

Mix together
- ¼ stick butter, melted
- juice of 2 limes
- 1 T. mustard (Dijon)
- pinch of fennel

"To eliminate odors from handling seafood, rub hands with lemon wedges or dried mustard."

Trout or Channel Bass

Serves 6

Arrange 2 lbs. of fillets cut in serving pieces in greased baking dish.

Mix together
- ¼ c. melted butter
- 1 t. salt
- 1 t. grated onion
- 1 t. paprika
- 2 T. lime juice
- dash of pepper

Pour this over fish and bake at 350° for 20 minutes.

Dolphin Fish

Place steaks in a baking dish, leaving some room between each one.

Pour herbed garlic salad dressing over them. Use ½ c. or so of the dressing. Marinate several hours turning every 30 minutes.

Grate sharp cheese and combine with equal amount of crushed cornflake crumbs. Roll the dolphin steaks in this mixture, coating evenly. Top steaks with remaining cheese and crumbs and bake at 450° for 15-20 minutes. Serve immediately.

Baked Red Snapper

Clean fish, leaving on the head and the tail.

Along each side make two or three diagonal slices. Put thin lemon and butter slices in each slit. Salt and pepper the fish. Bake at 350° until flaky.

Baked Flounder, Grouper, Spottail, Trout

Clean and behead fish; remove fins and tail.

Fish is moister and tastier if it is baked with bones intact. The meat separates from the bones with ease if it is cooked properly.

Place fish on sheet of foil in roasting pan. Rub cavity and outside with French dressing of your choice.

Wrap loosely with the foil, and place in preheated 425° oven. Bake for 25 minutes for small fish to 45 minutes for larger ones. Practice will help! Test by removing from oven, turning back the foil, and piercing with a fork. If flesh is white and firm, it is done. Usually the skin will split when it is done.

Remove to plates, garnish with parsley and lemon. Serve HOT.

"Left-over cooked fish can be frozen for later use in soups, stews, and chowders."

Smoked Mullet

"This is a delicious way to cook trout, bass, flounder, . . . and probably many others as well."

Make a fire in the grill using charcoal and hickory chips. Allow the coals to turn white and burn down some. Then cover the grill with a sheet of heavy aluminum foil. Place cleaned fish on the foil and on each fish put butter, lemon juice, salt, pepper, and a dash of oregano. Cover fish with grill lid or with another sheet of foil. Smoke until fish is flaky.

Basic Fried Fish

Coat fish with milk or beaten egg. Dredge in mixture of salted corn meal and flour. Fry in hot oil. Drain. Serve hot with lemon wedges and one of our sauces (page 80).

Bobbie's Buttermilk Fillets

Soak in buttermilk { Flounder, grouper, bass
15 minutes   { or trout fillets

Turn and soak another 15 minutes.

Dredge fish in lightly salted Bisquick. Fry or saute in oil or butter.

Hushpuppy Variation: Combine left-over buttermilk and Bisquick to batter consistency. Add sugar. Deep fat fry by the spoonfuls for delicious hushpuppies.

Shark Fillets

"Can be cooked the same as any bony fish"

1. Behead, deskin and degut shark. (Avoid breaking the guts open.)
2. Soak fresh shark in 1 gallon of ice water to which 1 cup of salt has been added.
3. Use shark within a day of catching or freeze in air-tight containers.
4. Cut into inch-thick steaks, chunks, etc.
5. Bake, fry, smoke, broil, etc. (see pages 30-35)

Savory Skate Wings

"Delicately flavored relative of the shark"

1. Rinse in cold water.
2. Cut into steaks, chunks or strips.
3. Blanch in boiling water.
4. Scrape the skin off.
5. Cook the same as you would any bony fish (pages 30-35)

French Fried Eel
(½ pound per person)

1. Behead and degut eel.
2. Nail the eel to a board for skinning.
3. Cut into bite size pieces.
4. Wash thoroughly.
5. Flour, salt and pepper or batter each piece.
6. Deep-fat fry until flaky and golden brown.
7. Serve with one of our sauces (p. 80) and lemon wedges.

"Beware of the bones."

Boiled Shrimp

"Boiled shrimp are done when they turn pinkish-white and become opaque."

Steve's Way

1. Fill dutch oven over halfway with water.
2. Add 13 oz. catsup, ½ c. vinegar, 1 or 2 bay leaves, and black pepper.
3. Bring to a boil. Then turn burner low and let simmer 10-15 minutes.
4. Add raw, unpeeled shrimp and cover. Simmer about 5 minutes or until pink. Drain.

Bevie's Method

1. Place peeled or unpeeled shrimp in pot and cover with cold water. Add salt and pepper. Sauer's or Rex's Seafood Seasoning may also be added.
2. Bring to a boil. *Immediately* remove from heat and drain in colander. Lightly rinse in cold water.

Boiled in Beer

1. Pour beer in pot and bring to a boil.
2. Add shrimp and cook until pink.

One 14 oz. can of beer should cook 2 lbs. shrimp.

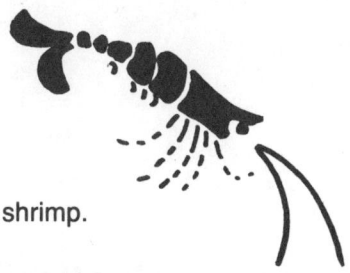

"Boil shrimp with their heads on if you want extra flavor."

Parboiled Shrimp

Drop peeled, deveined shrimp into boiling water by spoonfuls. Remove with slotted spoon <u>as soon as shrimp turn pink</u> (about one minute). Set aside to use in casseroles or other recipes.

Steamed Shrimp

Follow directions for Crab Crack (p. 57) substituting shrimp and varying amount of seasoning. Steam 'til shrimp turn pink.

"Add fresh celery leaves to boiling shrimp to absorb some of the odors."

Sauteed Creek Shrimp
"Incredible served over grits."

Peel and devein 1 lb. of shrimp. Saute in 1 stick of butter, about 8 to 10 minutes. Remove shrimp. Stir into the butter 1 T. lemon or lime juice, a dash of salt and a dash of pepper. Pour over the shrimp and serve immediately.

Broiled Rock Shrimp
"Rock shrimp will lose their flavor and texture if overcooked."

Split shrimp in half lengthwise through the midline of the top shell. Devein and rinse under water. Place the split side up on the broiling pan and brush with Lemon-Parsley-Butter Sauce (p. 81). Broil 3-5 minutes, no more. Serve with additional heated sauce.

Seafood Sauces page 80.

Sally's Fried Shrimp

"Beer Battered"

Peel shrimp back to the tail section. Leave tail for handling.

Mix together { ¼ c. flour
1 c. yellow corn meal
2 T. baking powder
⅛ c. sugar

Add beer to thicken to a consistency of pancake batter. Dip shrimp in batter and fry in hot grease. Drain.

Hushpuppy Variation: Add more cornmeal, chopped bell pepper and onion to this batter. Drop by the spoonfuls into hot grease and fry until golden brown.

"Don't forget to eat the crispy tails of fried fish and shrimp."

Made Dish of Shrimp and Crab

"May be frozen for later use."

Serves 10

Blend in a large bowl until smooth
{ 2 - 10½ oz. cans condensed cream of shrimp soup or equivalent of Harris Atlantic Shrimp Bisque
½ c. mayonnaise

Add
{ 1 med. onion, grated
¾ c. milk

Generously season to taste with
{ various salts
pepper
ground nutmeg
cayenne pepper

Combine above with
{ 3 lbs. shrimp, peeled, deveined and parboiled (p. 37)
1 - 6½ oz. can crab meat, drained
1 - 5 oz. can water chestnuts, drained and sliced thin
1½ c. celery, diced
4 T. fresh parsley, minced
1⅓ c. uncooked white long-grain rice, cooked until fluffy. (Add more rice to stretch the recipe.)

Check seasonings again. Add more milk if the mixture seems too dry. Place mixture in a large, shallow buttered casserole. Sprinkle with paprika and slivered almonds or Parmesan cheese. Bake uncovered at 350° for 30 minutes or until hot and bubbly. This can be made ahead and frozen, but be sure to use fresh shrimp since they should not be frozen twice.

"To make a small amount of shrimp go further in a casserole, split large fat shrimp in half lengthwise from end to end."

Bevie's Shrimp Thermidor

*"This recipe was the first enjoyed and exchanged by the editors of **Fripp Island Fare**, our original seafood cookbook."*

Serves 4

Saute 5 minutes
: { ½ c. fresh mushrooms, sliced
  ¼ c. butter, melted

Stir and blend
: { ¼ c. flour
  1 t. salt
  ½ t. dry mustard
  dash cayenne

Add 2 c. milk and cook, stirring constantly, until thickened.

Stir in ¾ lb. cooked shrimp, peeled and deveined.

Transfer to 6 ramekins or 1½ qt. casserole. Sprinkle with grated Parmesan cheese and paprika. Bake at 400° for 10 minutes.

Tangy Shrimp

Peel 2 lbs. of shrimp leaving on the tails.

Cook together
: { ¼ c. olive oil
  2 t. salt
  ½ t. white pepper

Place the shrimp in this mixture and cook until shrimp turn pink, about 3 to 5 minutes.

Combine
: { 2 T. lemon or lime juice
  ¼ c. dry vermouth

Add this to the shrimp, increasing the heat and cook 1 minute longer, stirring constantly.

Greek Style Shrimp

Serves 6

Place in sauce pan
and heat thoroughly
{ ½ c. olive oil
½ c. lemon juice
2 cloves garlic, mashed
¼ t. oregano

Place 2 lbs. cleaned, raw, extra large shrimp on broiling platter and pour mixture over shrimp. Broil on middle rack in oven until shrimp are done.

Ruth's Shrimp Scampi

Serves 4

Mix
{ 4 cloves garlic, crushed
2 t. salt
1 t. dry mustard
¼ t. pepper
4 T. parsley
6 t. lemon juice
½ c. olive oil

Add 2 lbs. of cleaned, raw shrimp.

Cover and marinate in the refrigerator for at least 8 hours. Pour into baking dish and broil for 10 minutes.

Shrimp and Japanese Vegetables

Serves 2

Cook and clean 1 lb. of shrimp. Cook as directed one package of Bird's Eye Japanese Vegetables. Add the shrimp and cook until warm throughout. Serve this over rice.

Shrimp and Chinese Vegetables

Serves 4

Cook and clean 2 lbs. of shrimp.

Saute minced garlic clove in 3 T. oil. Add shrimp and stir well. Add 1 T. sherry. Cook another 2 minutes. Remove shrimp to dish. Add a little more oil to saucepan and heat the oil. Add one package of Chinese vegetables and 1 jar of mushrooms. Cook just a few minutes. Blend 2 T. cornstarch to ½ c. chicken broth. Add the shrimp and vegetables to this mixture and stir until thickened. Serve this over rice with chow mein noodles.

Shrimp/Fish/Chicken Tempura

Mix
{ 1 egg yolk
2 c. ice water
⅛ t. baking soda

Add
{ 1⅔ c. plain flour

Blend with a wooden spoon and use immediately. If too thick, thin batter with ice water. Coat meat with batter. Fry in hot grease 'til golden brown and crispy.

Frogmore Goulash

"Frogmore is the 'capital' of St. Helena Island, South Carolina."

Serves 5 to 105*

Boil in dutch oven 10-15 mintues, allowing enough water to cover ingredients.	{ 1 large onion, chopped 1 large bell pepper, chopped 3 celery stalks, chopped 2 T. Old Bay Seasoning salt and pepper
Add and boil 10 minutes	{ hot Polish sausage cut in 1½ inch pieces
Add and boil 5-10 minutes	{ corn on the cob, broken in half
Add and boil 2-3 minutes	{ raw, unpeeled shrimp

Remove from heat, cover and let stand 4-5 minutes. Drain in colander.

*Allow at least ¾ lb. shrimp, 1 ear corn and 6 inches sausage per person.

"Reserve stock to be frozen and used in a bouillabaise or fish stew."

Bar-B-Que Shrimp

Serves 4

Bring to a boil 1¾ qts. vinegar.

Stir in	{ ¼ can dry mustard ¼ can red pepper ½ box celery seed

Add 5 lbs. shrimp. When water returns to a boil, cook for 5 minutes. Remove from burner. Let stand covered for five minutes.

Serve with plenty of saltines and dill pickles.

"The fastest way to clean 'a mess a shrimp' is to let each person clean his own."

Carolina Shrimp Casserole

Serves 6-8

Early in day
{ Cook 2½ lbs. shrimp (peeled and deveined) in boiling, salted water for 5 minutes. Drain. Place in 2 qt. casserole. Sprinkle with 1 T. lemon juice and 3 T. salad oil. Cook ¾ c. rice (or 1 c. precooked rice). Refrigerate both.

One hour, 10 minutes before serving:

Preheat oven to 350° and reserve 8-10 shrimp for garnish.

Saute for 5 minutes
{ 2 T. butter
¼ c. green pepper, minced
¼ c. onion, minced

Add and toss well
{ cooked rice
1 t. salt
⅛ t. pepper
⅛ t. mace
dash cayenne pepper
1 can tomato soup, undiluted
1 c. heavy cream
½ c. sherry
½ c. slivered blanched almonds

Bake uncovered 35 minutes. Then top with whole shrimp and ¼ c. almonds. Bake 20 minutes longer or until mixture is bubbly and shrimp is slightly browned.

Basic Shrimp Salad

Mix to taste
{
boiled shrimp
bell pepper
boiled eggs
chopped celery
mayonnaise or salad dressing
garlic salt
salt, pepper
}

Variations: A good way to stretch your salad is by adding cooked macaroni noodles or diced potatoes to this recipe.

Avocados Stuffed with Shrimp in Remoulade Sauce

8 servings

Combine in bowl
{
¼ c. tarragon vinegar
2 T. horseradish mustard
1 T. catsup
1½ t. paprika
½ t. salt
¼ t. cayenne pepper
}

Slowly add while beating { ½ c. salad oil.

Stir in
{
¼ c. celery, minced
¼ c. green onion and tops, minced
}

Pour remoulade over 2 lbs. cleaned, cooked shrimp. Marinate in refrigerator for 4-5 hours.

Cut 4 medium avocados in half and peel. Remove shrimp from sauce with slotted spoon and place on avocado halves. Arrange on platter with asparagus spears, cold sliced beets, hard-boiled egg slices. Additional remoulade sauce or a French dressing may be served with the shrimp.

Variation: This recipe may also be served as an appetizer.

Alligator Pears and Creek Shrimp Salad

"Makes an exceptional presentation dish."

Serves 4

Prepare { 2 alligator pears (avocados)

Cut in half, removing pit and peeling. Soak in lemon juice to prevent darkening.

Mix together {
- 2 c. boiled, peeled creek shrimp or 2 c. large shrimp cut in ¼" pieces
- 1 c. thinly sliced celery
- 1 c. diced pineapple (1 - 9 oz. can pineapple slices)
- ⅔ c. sour cream
- 1 t. onion salt

Chill until firm. Arrange pear halves on lettuce leaves and spoon mixture onto halves.

Cover with { 1 c. shredded Swiss cheese

Chill until ready to serve.

≲ *Cover fresh shrimp, shelled and deveined if desired, with cold water when freezing to maintain their outstanding taste.*

Quick Shrimp Creole

"Excellent beach recipe since the ingredients are usually on hand."

Serves 4

Saute
: pimientos
: bell pepper
: onions

Add
: 1 - 15 oz. can tomato sauce
: 1 sm. can tomato paste

Ten minutes before serving, add 1 lb. peeled raw shrimp. Serve over rice. The sauce part may be made as much as a week ahead of time and refrigerated. Then heat when needed and add shrimp.

It may be necessary to thin sauce with a small amount of water. It may also be spiced up by adding hot sauce, worcestershire, basil, oregano, garlic, or any combination of these ingredients.

Creole Shrimp Bake

"This freezes well and may be made ahead of time when one is serving a mob of people."

Serves 8-10

Saute in butter until clear
: ½ c. celery, chopped
: 1 large onion, chopped
: ½ c. green pepper, chopped

Combine with
: 1 c. raw rice
: ¾ lb. grated sharp cheese
: 1 T. worcestershire
: 1 large can sliced mushrooms & juice
: 1 large can tomato sauce
: salt & pepper to taste
: 3 lbs. peeled, raw shrimp

Turn into greased casserole and top with ¼ lb. grated sharp cheese. Bake at 350° for about 45 minutes or until hot. Stir occasionally while baking. Add water and/or cover if creole looks dry.
When using large shrimp you may want to cut them in half.

Shrimp Creole with Cheese Rice

Serves 6-8

In large skillet cook until clear:
- ½ c. chopped bacon
- 2 cloves chopped garlic
- ⅔ c. celery, chopped
- 1 large onion, chopped
- 1 med. bell pepper, chopped
- ½ c. olive oil

Add these to above:
- 1 large can Spanish tomatoes
- 2 - 6 oz. cans tomato paste
- 1 c. water
- 1½ t. sugar
- 2 t. worcestershire
- ½ t. tabasco
- salt and pepper to taste

Let mixture come to a boil and let simmer for 3 hours. Ten minutes before serving, add 2½ lbs. of cleaned, raw shrimp. Serve with cheese rice.

Cheese rice:
Chop 1 onion very fine and cook this in the water in which you are cooking your rice. When rice is done, grate 1 c. sharp cheddar cheese and stir into rice until melted. Make a ring of your rice on a large platter and place creole in the center.

Marcia's Shrimp Creole

"Excellent vacation recipe."

Serves 4

Saute until tender:
- 4 T. oil
- 2 medium onions, chopped
- 1 bell pepper, chopped
- 1½ c. celery, chopped

Add and simmer:
- 2 cans tomato soup
- 1 t. sugar
- 1 t. salt
- hot sauce

then add 1 lb. peeled, raw shrimp and stir constantly. Let simmer again for a few minutes. Serve on rice.

Old House Creek Shrimp and Brown Gravy

Serves 4

Cook until clear
Remove and drain.
- 4 T. bacon grease
- 2 onions, sliced
- 2 green peppers, sliced

Brown in bacon grease.
Remove. Drain.
- 2 lbs. peeled shrimp, floured

Mix with grease. Make a thick brown gravy.
- flour and water, shaken together
- salt
- pepper
- worcestershire
- dash of soy sauce

Add. Heat thoroughly.
Serve over rice or grits.
- onions
- peppers
- shrimp
- crab meat (optional)

Shrimp are easier to peel while partially frozen.

Fripp Island Shrimp Curry

"This recipe rates '5 STARS' by the editors."

Serves 6-8

Saute and let simmer
{ 4 T. butter
1 large onion, chopped fine
½ c. apple, chopped fine
½ c. celery, chopped fine

Add and let simmer until most of the stock has cooked away
{ 1½ c. chicken stock or chicken bouillon

Stir in
{ ¼ t. ginger
¼ c. raisins
salt and pepper
1 T. lemon juice
2 T. curry powder

Add 1 pt. cream and cook gently until cream is reduced to sauce consistency. (If milk is substituted for cream, add 2 c. milk and thicken with a flour paste made of several T. flour mashed into butter.) After it has thickened, add 3 lbs. parboiled or raw shrimp and heat thoroughly.

The first stage of this recipe may be made earlier in the day, leaving the shrimp to be added just before serving.

Serve the curry over rice with assorted condiments such as raisins, coconut, chopped peanuts and Major Grey's Chutney.

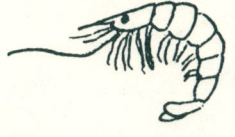

"To make a small amount of shrimp go further in a casserole, split large fat shrimp horizontally."

Seafood Casserole

"Outstanding over rice."

Serves 6-8

Saute; remove with slotted spoon to cool	1½ sticks butter 1 large onion, chopped 1 green pepper, chopped 4 sticks celery, chopped
Mix and sprinkle into butter in pan	4 T. flour ¼ t. dry mustard ¼ t. powdered thyme 1¼ t. marjoram
Add and stir until it starts to thicken	1 pt. cream 4 or 5 dashes tabasco 1 T. worcestershire
Stir in until melted	1 jar very sharp cheese 1 pt. mushrooms salt & pepper
Add and simmer for 5 minutes	2 lbs. raw cleaned shrimp 1 lb. crab meat

Serve hot from chafing dish or casserole topped with parsley and chives.

Lowcountry Paella

"Use any combination of shrimp, chicken, pork chops, clams, etc."

Serves 6

Brown chicken or meat in peanut oil and drain.

Cut bell pepper in 1" strips and fry. Put aside to drain.

Fry
{
- 1 clove garlic, peeled and chopped
- 2 large tomatoes, blended in mixer or 1 sm. can tomato sauce
}

Add
{
- 2 c. water
- 1 c. clam juice or liquid from canned peas
- 1 large onion, chopped
}

Bring to a boil; then turn low and put meat back in. Cook for 15 minutes.

Add
{
- pinch saffron
- salt & pepper
- can of peas
- 1 c. raw rice
- uncooked shrimp, peeled and deveined
- clams in shells (well scrubbed)
}

Turn heat up to boiling. *DO NOT STIR.* Let cook 15 to 20 minutes.

Turn heat off and take pan off burner. Let sit until rice soaks up liquid. Place pepper strips on top and serve.

> In 1520 the first Europeans (Spaniards) landed on what is now Beaufort, S.C. Live oaks bearded with Spanish moss remind today's tourists and residents of their struggle to take hold and survive in a new land.

Shrimp and Crab Panama

Serves 6

Saute until tender
{ 1 c. chopped onion
1 c. chopped green pepper
1 c. thinly sliced celery

Add and heat
{ 2 cans frozen cream of shrimp soup, thawed*
¼-½ c. diced pimiento
1 lb. crab meat
salt & pepper

Add and heat, **do not let boil**
{ 1 c. sour cream

Serve over rice. Extra shrimp can be added if desired.

Variation: Make a white sauce and add shrimp if the frozen cream of shrimp soup is not available.

Crab-Shrimp Casserole

"This is absolutely delicious hot! May also be used cold as stuffing for a tomato or as a salad on a bed of lettuce."

Serves 4

Combine and place in casserole dish
{ ⅓ medium green pepper, chopped
⅓ medium onion, chopped
⅔ c. celery, diced
large soup bowl of fresh crab meat
¾ lb. shrimp, cleaned and cooked
½ t. salt
⅛ t. pepper
1 T. worcestershire
4 drops tabasco
⅛ to ¼ c. mayonnaise
4 oz. cream cheese

Sprinkle with 1 c. buttered bread crumbs. Bake at 350° for 30 minutes.

Port Royal Shrimp and Wild Rice

"This dish can be made earlier in the day and is simply delicious for a family get-together."

Serves 6

Saute and remove to large bowl	{ 3 T. butter 3 T. green pepper, chopped 3 T. onion, chopped
Saute in butter until pink	{ 2½ lbs. raw, peeled shrimp
Sprinkle the shrimp with	{ ½ t. salt
Combine	{ 1 can cream of mushroom soup 1½ T. lemon juice 1½ t. worcestershire ½ t. dry mustard ½ t. pepper ½ c. cheddar cheese, cubed 1 pkg. wild rice cooked

Mix well with shrimp, peppers, and onions. Bake in casserole at 350° for 35 minutes.

Shrimp and Rice Casserole

4-5 servings

Cook 1 c. rice according to package directions.

Saute	{ 2 med. onions, chopped ½ c. butter
Add and heat	{ 1 lb. raw shrimp, peeled and deveined 1 - 1 lb. can tomatoes cayenne pepper 1 t. salt ½ t. paprika ⅛ t. mace (opt.) 1 t. worcestershire

Stir in rice. Place mixture in shallow 2 qt. (12 x 8 x 2) baking dish. Arrange 4 slices bacon (cut in halves) on top. Bake uncovered at 375° for 30 minutes.

Crabs

Cooking and Cleaning Method #1

1. Put 1 inch of water into a pot.
2. Add 3 T. vinegar, 3 T. salt and a couple of bay leaves.
3. When water boils, add *live* crabs.
4. Boil, or steam on a rack, for 25-30 minutes.
5. Drain crabs in the sink and let them get cool.
6. Pull back tongue (male crab) or apron (female crab) by inserting a knife to loosen it.
7. Break off legs and claws at the body.
8. Remove shells from the body and discard.
9. Remove the "dead man" (feathery gills) and "glop" (digestive organs) from the body cavity. "This should be done over newspaper or over the sink."
10. Rinse thoroughly.
11. Using a nut cracker and nut pick, remove the meat from the body, legs and claws. The body may be broken in half for easier picking.

Cleaning and Cooking Method #2

"Avoid the mealtime mess, crabs can be cleaned before you steam them."

1. Turn live crab belly-side up on a chopping block.
2. Grabbing the crab's hind legs, CAREFULLY break off the large claws with pliers. Steam these pinchers with the bodies and then try our Marinated Crab Claws p. 12.
3. Center a meat cleaver on the crab's body.
4. Hit the cleaver with a mallet, dividing the crab in half.
5. Remove the shells from the body and discard.
6. Clean crab cavity under running water, removing all of the "dead man" and "glop."
7. Place crabs in a seafood steamer or colander suspended over boiling water. Now follow Jan's recipe for a "Civilized Crab Crack," next page.

No Fuss Method #3

"Avoid all the cookin', cleanin' and pickin' . . . buy Harris Atlantic Crab Meat" available in most local grocery stores or from Blue Channel Company. Please refer to pages 93 and 94.

Seafood Sauces page 80.

Jan's Civilized Crab Crack

Clean live crabs according to Method #2 on page 56.

Step 8. Add 2 T. Old Bay Seasoning.
Step 9. Cover and steam about 20 minutes or until meat is firm and flaky.
Step 10. Serve with Lemon-Parsley-Butter Sauce page 84.

> *"Served picked crab meat with drawn butter or one of our cocktail sauces on page 80."*

Boiled Crabs — "The Chinese Way"

Boil crabs whole with joint of fresh ginger root. . . . Adds a new dimension to a crab crack.

Soft-Shell Crab

> *"Pierce soft shell crabs several times before frying to prevent the grease from popping."*

Crab must be used immediately so that shell won't harden. If it is to be used at a later date, put in plastic bag and freeze. Thaw in salty water to maintain flavor.

Lift up tips of shell and remove all glop. If crab is to be frozen, cut off spines so that they will not puncture plastic bag. Cut face off with a knife.

Dip crab in beaten egg. Salt and pepper them. Roll in flour and/or cornmeal mixture. Deep fat fry in hot oil until golden-brown. Drain and serve hot.

Variation: Left-over fried soft-shell crabs may be chilled and served in a sandwich with tartare sauce.

Deviled Crab I

Make a white sauce of
{ ¼ stick oleo blended with
2 T. flour, then add
1 c. milk and stir until thick

Mix together and blend with white sauce
{ ¼ lb. crushed saltines
1 bell pepper, chopped
3 heaping T. catsup
1 beaten egg
1 t. prepared mustard
1 T. (full) worcestershire
1 T. hot sauce
salt
½ stick melted butter
2 c. crab meat

Place in individual oiled serving shells or greased casserole. Top with cracker crumbs. Bake at 350° until lightly browned (about 30 minutes).

"Deviled crab can be placed on styrofoam meat trays for easy freezing, then covered with freezer wrap. This keeps the tips of the shells from poking through . . so save your styrofoam containers."

Deviled Crab II

Serves 6-8

Mix together
{ 2 c. crab meat
4 hard-cooked eggs, mashed
3 T. mayonnaise
2 T. lemon juice
1 T. worcestershire
1 T. dry mustard
salt & pepper
2 c. toasted bread crumbs

Place in well-greased baking dish and heat in oven.

Crab Stuffed Potatoes

Bake 4 baking potatoes. Scoop out insides and . . .

Mix with electric mixer on low speed {
- 1 stick butter
- ½ c. sour cream
- 1 t. salt
- 4 t. grated onion
- 1 c. grated cheese
- 6 t. paprika

Whip for 1 minute after thoroughly blended.

Add 1 - 6½ oz. can crab meat and mix with a fork.

Fill potatoes with mixture and sprinkle with paprika. Reheat in 450° oven about 15 minutes.

{
- 1-6½ oz. can yields about ¾ cup
- 2-6½ oz. cans yield meat from about 10 crabs
- 3-6½ oz. cans yield just over 1 pound

Basic Crab Casserole

Combine {
- meat from 10 crabs (about 2 cans)
- ¾ c. crushed saltines
- bell pepper strips
- onion
- pimiento
- garlic
- ½ can cream of mushroom soup
- ½ c. grated cheese (opt.)
- hard-boiled egg slices (opt.)
- hot sauce (opt.)

Bake about 30 minutes at 400°. This makes a colorful dish with the pimiento slices and green pepper strips. The amount of pepper, onion, etc., can be varied to suit personal taste.

Variations: Substitute one beaten egg for the boiled egg and increase the soup and saltines to one cup each. Add ½ stick melted butter.

Summertime Crab Casserole

Combine:
- 1 lb. crab meat
- 5 pieces hard toast, biscuits or cornbread
- ¼ c. minced celery that has been sauteed in 2 T. butter
- 1 stick butter
- 3 eggs
- 1 c. hot water
- juice of one lemon
- salt & pepper
- worcestershire
- tabasco

At the very last add ½ t. baking powder and bake at 350° until bubbly. Sprinkle some paprika on top of the casserole before baking.

Crab Meat Imperial

Serves 4

Mix together:
- 1 lb. fresh lump crab meat
- ½ t. salt
- ⅛ t. cayenne pepper
- 3 T. mayonnaise
- 2 dashes worcestershire
- 1 T. chopped parsley

Use fork and be careful to avoid breaking up the lumps of crab meat when mixing.

Place in pastry shells and top with a pat of butter. Sprinkle with paprika. Bake at 375° for 15 minutes or until hot and golden brown.

Sea Island Crab Sandwich

"A meal in itself"   Satisfies 4 people

Combine and blend all ingredients
{
- 2 - 6½ oz. cans Harris Atlantic Claw Crab Meat, rinsed
- ½ c. mayonnaise
- ⅓ c. sour cream
- ⅓ c. celery, chopped
- ¼ T. pimiento, chopped
- 1 T. lemon juice
- ½ t. garlic salt

Slice one loaf of French or Italian bread the long way on one side only. Hollow the loaf by removing some of the insides. Stuff the loaf with the crab mixture. Bake in a 350° oven until lightly browned, about 25 minutes. Just before removing from the oven, top with Swiss cheese slices.

Congealed Crab Salad

Mix together
{
- 1 pkg. plain gelatin
- ¾ c. water

Heat slowly and stir 3 minutes until gelatin is dissolved.

Add and stir
{
- 2 T. lemon juice
- 1 c. mayonnaise
- 1 c. crab meat
- ¼ c. onion, minced
- ⅓ c. celery, sliced
- ⅓ c. green pepper, chopped
- dash of tabasco, mustard, and worcestershire

Pour into molds or bowls and chill. This is nice garnished with hard-boiled egg slices and fresh tomato slices. If placed in individual bowls, it will be set in about 30 minutes.

Variation: Tuna may be substituted for crab meat.

Seafood Omelets

Serves 2

Basic Omelet:

Beat until blended
- 5 eggs
- 2 T. water
- ½ t. salt
- ⅛ t. pepper

Heat omelet pan or skillet over heat for one minute. Add 2 T. butter and tilt pan to cover sides and bottom. When foam subsides, add omelet mixture.

Cook over medium heat, shaking pan gently back and forth. Lift edges of egg mixture with rubber spatula while tilting pan so that uncooked egg will flow to bottom. Cook until set and bottom is slightly browned. Slide onto plate, fill, and fold in half.

Seafood Toppings:

Shrimp Creole Sauces page 48
Crab Meat Filling and Cheese Sauce page 63
Thickened Tidalholm Seafood Chowder page 24

Crab Meat Quiche

Mix together
- 4 wedges Gruyere cheese, grated
- ½ c. sour cream
- ½ c. mayonnaise
- 1 t. salt
- 1 t. worcestershire
- ½ c. onion, chopped
- 1 - 6½ oz. can crab meat

Bake pastry shell 5 minutes. Spoon mixture into shell and bake at 350° for 45 minutes. Let sit until firm.

Variation: Cheddar and/or Swiss cheese may be used instead of Gruyere.

Margaret's Crab Meat Crepes

Crepe Recipe:

Beat one egg to blend.

Add { 1¼ c. milk
1 T. butter, melted
1¼ c. flour (all-purpose)
½ t. salt

Beat until smooth. Additional milk may be added if batter seems too thick. Pour ladleful of batter into lightly greased skillet or crepe pan and tilt pan so that batter covers the bottom. Brown on one side and remove from pan. Continue until batter is used up. Makes 8 crepes.

Crab Meat Filling:

Saute in butter { 1 lb. crab meat
1 shallot, chopped
½ green pepper, sliced
pimiento strips
clove of garlic, crushed
hot sauce or cayenne
salt and pepper

Cheese Sauce:

Make a cream sauce of 2 T. butter, 2 T. flour, and 1 c. milk.

Add & blend well { 4 oz. grated cheddar or Swiss cheese
1 t. grated onion and juice, or
 chopped green onion
½ can mushrooms
salt & peper

Place crab meat mixture in center of crepe and fold edges over. Spoon cheese sauce over each.

Anita's Crab Casserole

"The first part of this recipe makes a delicious crab salad."

Mix
{
- 2 lb. crab meat (amount can be varied)
- 1 c. celery, chopped
- 1 medium onion, chopped
- 1 c. mayonnaise*
- 1 T. mustard
- salt & paprika, mixed
- green pepper (optional)
- pimiento (optional)

Spread over trimmed bread slices in greased casserole. Top with Velveeta cheese slices. If deep casserole is used, mixture can be divided and two layers made.

Combine.
{
- 2 eggs, beaten
- 1 c. milk
- dash of worcestershire

Pour over casserole and bake at 325° for 35-45 minutes. Casserole should be bubbly.

*Amount of mayonnaise can be varied in accordance with amount of crab meat used.

Sauteed Crab Meat Plantation

Serves 4-6

Saute until soft
- ¼ c. green onion, minced
- ¼ c. green pepper, minced
- 4 oz. bacon, minced
- 1 oz. salt pork, minced
- 2 oz. clarified butter

Add and saute 1 min. while stirring
- 1 lb. crab meat
- dash of worcestershire, salt, and white pepper

At 1 minute intervals, add the following ingredients in order. Stir after each addition.
- 2 oz. white wine (Chablis)
- 1 c. hot chicken stock
- 2 eggs, beaten

Combine
- ¼ c. cracker meal
- ⅛ c. Parmesan cheese

Blend with crab meat mixture. Sprinkle ⅛ c. of Parmesan cheese over the top and place under broiler. Brown evenly. Serve with lemon wedges.

"Keep all seafood cooled on ice or in the coldest part of the refrigerator."

"Clams may be frozen in their shells by placing them in the freezer in paper bags. They will pop open and can easily be removed for use in recipes."

Steamed Clams

1. Scrub clams well under cold water.

2. Place in large dutch oven and add 1 c. water.

3. Cover and place over high heat. Check every five minutes until clams are thoroughly opened.

When steaming a large amount of clams, use roasting pan. Place clams in roaster with 1 c. water. Cover and place in 500° oven until clams pop open.

Variations: Clam juice (liquor) or broth is delicious served hot in mugs with a pat of butter or it may be saved to use in other recipes.

Clams Steamed in Wine

Combine { 1 c. water
          { 1 c. dry white wine

Steam until clams open. Take top off the broth and save for chowders and other dishes. It will keep for several weeks in the refrigerator or may be frozen for future use. See variations above.

See page 80 for cocktail sauces.

Reese's Clam Delight

"Smells as good as it tastes."

Scrub clam shells well in cold water. Steam clams in ½ c. white wine and ½ c. water until clams open.

Remove from shells, reserving shells.

Combine
{
¼ lb. butter
2 t. crushed parsley
¼ t. chervil
1 onion, finely chopped
2 garlic buds, minced
salt & pepper to taste
MSG
}

Place 2 clams in each half-shell with butter paste. (This can be done a few days in advance and kept in the refrigerator.)

Sprinkle top of clams with grated mozzarella and Parmesan cheese and bake in 400° oven until bubbly.

Serve with French bread to "sop up all that good butter."

Clam Fritters

Serves 4-6

Beat { 1 egg

Add and mix well
{
1 c. ground fresh or frozen clams
1 small onion, chopped (the more the better)
1 c. flour
salt and pepper to taste
½ t. sugar
}

Fold in { 1 heaping t. baking powder

Drop heaping teaspoonfuls of the mixture into hot (deep) grease. Fry one fritter, drain and taste to see if more seasonings, clam liquor, or milk needs to be added before frying the rest. Serve hot.

Clam Sauce for Pasta

Saute until soft
{ 4 T. butter
½ minced onion
1 clove garlic
½ lb. minced clams or
    1 can minced clams }

Add 2 T. flour to make a paste.

Combine with above
{ 1 c. clam juice
2 T. parsley
dash cayenne pepper
salt and white pepper }

You may find that you need more clam juice to stretch the sauce. Serve this over the pasta.

Clam Spaghetti

Combine
{ 1 c. meat stock
1 c. tomato puree
1 clove garlic, minced
basil, oregano, parsley to taste
1 can minced clams and juice }

Simmer together for 30 minutes. Serve over spaghetti noodles.

Clam Linguine

Heat in frying pan
{ 3 T. olive oil
¼ lb. butter

Add
{ 2 crushed cloves garlic
1 t. oregano
2 T. parsley
dash of tabasco
black pepper
1 can of minced clams or fresh clams

Heat, then pour over and toss with linguine noodles.

Clam Linguine For 10

Bring to a boil one #5 can clam juice.

Thicken with cornstarch

Add and mix
{ 3 T. olive oil
6 garlic cloves, chopped
½ medium onion, chopped
5 shallots, chopped
7-8 anchovies, chopped

Add one #5 can clams, chopped

Season with
{ dash of worcestershire
tabasco
dash of Accent
4 T. parsley, chopped

Serve immediately over linguine noodles.

Roasted Oysters

1. Rinse oysters to get mud off.

2. Place metal (tin) sheet over hot fire (charcoal or wood).

3. Put oysters on the tin and cover with wet burlap sack. Periodically resoak bag so it will not dry out and burn.

4. Oysters are done when they pop open.

Serve with melted butter and/or cocktail sauces, page 80.

> In the 1660's William Hilton, after whom Hilton Head Island was named, explored the Carolina Sea Islands for future English settlements. Today the tourists, at Hilton Head and other neighboring islands, enjoy the outdoor oyster roasts in the cooler months "down South."

Fried Oysters

Dip oysters in beaten egg. Coat with seasoned half-flour/half-cornmeal mixture. Deep fat fry until golden brown. Drain.

OR

Follow same directions as for Sally's Fried Shrimp, page 39.

"Roll fresh oysters in cornmeal then freeze on styrofoam trays covered with freezer wrap. When you're hungry for fried oysters, just pop them frozen into deep fat and fry 'til golden brown."

Steamed Oysters

May be prepared as steamed clams, either on top of the stove or in oven.

Oyster Pie

Have on hand { drained raw oysters
saltine crackers (crumbled)
Parmesan cheese
butter
milk
salt and pepper

Cover bottom of shallow casserole dish with thin layer of cracker crumbs. Add layer of oysters. Dot with butter, salt and pepper. Continue layers with final layer of cracker crumbs. Sprinkle top with Parmesan cheese and add milk to come to top layer. Bake 350° 'til firm.

Scalloped Oysters

Saute 1 T. grated onion in 1 c. melted butter.

Combine above with { ½ c. liquid from oysters
2½ c. cracker crumbs
2 t. salt
2 t. pepper
1 T. lemon juice

In a 2 qt. casserole layer { 2 qt. oysters
crumb mixture

Pour ⅔ c. light cream over this. You may top this with cheese. Bake at 450° for 30 minutes.

Chicken and Oyster Dish

Serves 8

Have on hand
- 4 c. cooked deboned chicken
- 1 pint raw oysters
- oyster liquid plus chicken broth to make 4 cups

Saute until well-coated
- 1 T. butter
- 1 c. raw rice

Add 2 c. of the oyster/chicken liquid. Bring to a boil. Cover and simmer on low heat twenty minutes.

Saute 10 minutes
- 7 T. butter
- ½ lb. mushrooms, sliced

Remove from heat.

Pour over mushrooms
- 2 T. brandy

Ignite brandy and shake pan until flame dies. Sprinkle mushrooms with 6 T. flour and place over medium heat. Cook, stirring, 3 minutes.

Add
- 2 c. oyster/chicken liquid
- 1 c. rich milk or half and half

Cook and stir until thickened.

Season with
- salt
- freshly ground nutmeg

Layer in order in 3-4 qt. dish, repeating once
- 4 c. cooked chicken, large pieces
- rice
- 1 pt. raw oysters
- sauce

Cover with
- ½ c. bread crumbs
- ¼ c. fresh grated Parmesan cheese

Bake at 350° for 30 minutes.

John Hilliard's Pork Chops with Oyster Dressing

"The dressing is a dish in itself."

1-2 servings

Saute in 1 oz. clarified butter
{ ¼ c. minced onion
¼ c. minced bell pepper

Mix together
{ ¾ c. pure chicken stock, heated
¼ c. diced day-old bread
¼ c. diced cornbread
onions and peppers
½ c. raw diced, shucked oysters
¼ t. sage
¼ t. poultry seasoning
dash garlic salt, salt and white pepper

Heat the oyster dressing one to three minutes.

Stuff two 8 oz. center-cut pork chops (that have been trimmed and pocketed) with oyster dressing. Baste with 1 oz. clarified butter. Bake in 350°-375° oven for 20-25 minutes. Turn chops once after 15 minutes.

"You may find this recipe will be adequate for two servings, depending on the side dishes served with it."

Our Oysters Rockefeller

Combine { 1 pint raw oysters
¼-⅓ lb. fresh spinach, cooked & chopped (or 1 pkg. frozen)
½ stick butter
3 T. lemon juice
pepper
2-3 slices bread, crumbled in blender
8 drops hot sauce
minced onion
1 T. parsley flakes

This can be returned to the half-shell or baked in a casserole dish.

Top with { 1-2 wedges of Gruyere cheese, mozzarella, Swiss, etc.

Bake in 400° oven for 10 minutes.

Sauteed Scallops p. 16
Saviche Variation with Scallops p.6

Channel Conch and Whelk

"Collected from the mudflats or sandflats"

1. Scrub off the sand or mud.
2. Using a chisel or hammer, break off the tip of the conch's spiral.
3. Gently pry the animal out with an ice pick or screw driver. The remaining shell can be used as a horn, so do NOT throw it away.
4. Cut off the operculum (round trap door), digestive organs and any other spongy membranes.
5. Wash the animal thoroughly.
6. Cut into smaller chunks.
7. Bash each piece against a hard surface . . . the sidewalk will do just fine OR beat the flesh with a mallet to tenderize the muscle.
8. Rinse the "tenderized" conch with water.
9. Boil chunks in salted water, flavored with Old Bay Seasoning, for 20 or more minutes 'til "tender," OR marinate in lime juice, wine or other marinade 4 hours or overnight in refrigerator.
10. Cut each chunk into bite-size pieces or strips. Dip into hot butter or your favorite sauce (p. 80) OR dip into prepared batter (p. 82) and deep-fat fry if the critters still need more cooking. OR, for best results . . .
11. Grind the conch meat chunks and add to seafood chowders and stews the same as other mollusks. OR, you may want to try . . .
12. Conch Fritters . . . Follow the directions for Clam Fritters (p. 67), substituting ground conch.
13. Now, try to eat your conch concoction. Some say, "no matter what you do to conch, it still tastes like rubber." Good luck!

Fried Squid

Cleaning: *"If it takes you longer than 2 minutes, you need practice."*

1. Grabbing the eyes (quills), jerk the head out of the hood (mantle).
2. Yank everything else (intestines, etc.) out of the hood.
3. Throw away all of the innards, including the ink sac.
4. Cut off the tentacles.
5. Pop out the inedible horny tooth or beak near the tentacles.
6. Grab the transparent "pen" and attached membranes inside the hood. Remove and discard this.
7. Rub off and discard the speckled skin on the hood.
8. Wash the hood and tentacles thoroughly.

Cooking:

1. Cut hood and/or tentacles (better suited for soups and chowders) into 1-inch rings or strips.
2. Salt and pepper the pieces.
3. Dip pieces into flour or batter (p. 82).
4. Deep-fat fry (no more than 2 minutes on each side) 'til golden brown and cripsy. Drain.
5. Serve with lemon wedges.

Edible Octopus

1. Cut off all eight tentacles.
2. Rub or peel off the outer skin.
3. Cut tentacles into bite-size pieces.
4. Boil chunks in salty water about 20 minutes or longer, to tenderize.
5. Dip pieces into flour or prepared batter (p. 82)
6. Deep-fat fry. Drain.
7. Serve with cocktail sauces (p. 80).

YOUR SEAFOOD SECRETS

U.S. METRIC EQUIVALENTS

LIQUID VOLUME

	t.	ounce	pint	quart	ml.	liter
1 milliliter	.2	.034	.002	.001	1	.001
1 teaspoon (t.)	1	1/6	1/96	1/192	5	.005
1 dessertspoon	2	1/3	1/48	1/96	10	.010
1 tablespoon	3	1/2	1/32	1/64	15	.015
1 cup	48	8	1/2	1/4	236	.236
1 quart	192	32	2	1	946	.946
1 liter (l.)	203	34	2.1	1.057	1000	1.
1 gallon	768	128	8	4	3785	3.785

WEIGHT

	ounce	pound	milligram	gram	kilogram
1 gram	.032	.002	1000.	1.	.001
1 ounce	1	1/16	28,350.	28.35	.028
1 pound	16	1	453,600.	454.	.454
1 kilogram	.000032	2.2	1,000,000.	1000.	1.

TEMPERATURE

	Fahrenheit	Centigrade
Freezing	32°	0°
Boiling	212°	100°
	250° up	121° up
Baking	350° up	177° up
	450° up	232° up
Broiling	550° up	288° up

seafood sauces, etc.

Basic Cocktail Sauce

Mix ketchup and horseradish to taste. Add dash of lemon juice.

Cocktail Sauce

"to be served warm"

Mix together over medium heat.
- 1 stick butter, melted
- 1 bottle ketchup (13 oz. size)
- 3 t. horseradish
- 2 T. hot pepper sauce

Stir this constantly. Be sure ingredients are completely blended. Serve hot.

Cocktail Sauce for Shrimp

Mix together
- 1 c. mayonnaise
- 1 t. lemon juice
- 1 t. curry powder
- ½ t. minced onion
- ½ t. worcestershire
- ½ t. red pepper sauce
- ¼ c. chili sauce
- salt to taste
- pepper to taste

Mix well and keep in refrigerator until ready to serve.

Oyster Cocktail Sauce

Mix together
- 4 T. ketchup or chili sauce
- 2 t. lemon juice
- 1½ t. worcestershire
- dash of salt
- dash of pepper
- 1½ t. horseradish

Pour this over oysters just before serving.

Tartare Sauce

"Especially good with fried shrimp or your favorite fish."

Mix together
{
½ c. mayonnaise or salad dressing
1 t. sweet pickle relish or diced pickle
1 t. pickle juice or lemon juice
1 T. minced onion
dash of paprika, if desired
}

Variation: Add 1 t. prepared mustard.

Lemon-Parsley-Butter Sauce

"Use with most baked or broiled seafoods."

Mix well.
{
½ c. butter, melted
3 T. lemon juice
1 T. chopped parsley
Celery salt (optional)
Oregano (optional)
}

Remoulade Sauce p. 46

Cheese Sauce p. 63

Creole Sauces pp. 48-49

etc.

Hush Puppies

Mix together
{
1 c. self-rising corn meal
½ c. self-rising flour
1 t. sugar
⅛ t. soda
1 onion, chopped (optional)
}

Add *buttermilk* to make batter a little thicker than cake batter.

Carefully drop by teaspoonfuls into hot, deep fat. Fry until golden brown.

Variation: Try Bobbie's Buttermilk Hushpuppy Variation, page 35.
Try Sally's Hushpuppy Variation, page 39.

Seafood Batters

Many seafoods can be battered and fried. We suggest you try . . .
Sally's Beer Batter . . . . p. 39
Bobbie's Buttermilk Batter . . . . p. 35
Tempura Batter . . . . p. 43

Mary's Lemon Crumbs

"Tops almost any seafood"

Saute in butter
{
bread crumbs (any amount)
pecans or almonds, finely
  chopped (optional)
parsley, freshly chopped (optional)
}

Remove from heat and add { lemon peel, grated (any amount)

Mix well. Store in refrigerator or freezer. Sprinkle on favorite seafood or other dish before serving.

Geechee Grits

6 Servings

Follow cooking directions on the box to yield { 3 c. cooked grits (hominy)

Add to hot grits { 1 stick butter

In another bowl, mix well then add to hot buttered grits mixture { 3-4 eggs, well beaten
1 c. milk

Place mixture into a shallow casserole dish set in a pan of water. Bake one hour at 350°-375°.

Variation: Add grated cheese prior to baking.

> In the 1740's indigo replaced rice as the big money crop for the Sea Islands of South Carolina.

Rice St. Helena

"Colorful side dish with shrimp or fish"

Saute briefly each one of the following, one at a time. Set each aside. { fresh bell pepper wedges
onion strips or rings
peeled tomato wedges
sliced water chestnuts (optional)
slivered almonds (optional)

Toss with (warmed left-over) cooked rice.
Sprinkle with grated cheese (optional).

etc.

Dill Salad
"Goes well with most seafoods"

Combine. (Use any combination of colored vegetables to achieve the desired effect.)
- can large peas, drained
- can kidney beans or beets, drained
- can of sliced potatoes, drained
- can lima beans, drained
- can yellow wax beans, drained

Mix together. Pour over vegetables. Chill several hours.
- ½ c. mayonnaise
- ¼ c. onion, chopped
- 1 T. sugar
- 1 T. fresh dill, chopped = ½ t. dried
- 1 T. cider vinegar
- 1 t. dry mustard
- ¾ t. salt

Dot's Cole Slaw
"A Pawley's Island favorite"

Chop or grate
- 1 head cabbage
- 1 onion (optional)
- 1-3 stalks celery

Combine dressing. Mix with slaw. Chill several hours before serving to allow flavors to blend.
- 1 c. mayonnaise
- 2 T. cider vinegar
- 2 t. sugar (to taste)
- 1 t. salt (to taste)
- pepper (optional)
- poppy seeds (optional)

menus

menus

menus

BRUNCHES

—SUNDAY BRUNCH—

Bloody Mary
Marinated Raw Fresh Vegetables
Sautéed Creek Shrimp (p. 38) on Grits
Scrambled Eggs
Sliced Country Ham
Hot Biscuits   Jams   Butter
Coffee   Hot Tea

—LADIES BRUNCH—

Cold Carrot Soup
Shrimp Thermidor (p. 41) in shell ramekins
French-style Green Beans with Toasted Almonds
Hot Flaky Rolls   Butter
Creme de Menthe Parfait
White Wine   Coffee

LUNCHEONS

—BRIDGE LUNCHEON FOR FOUR—

Wine Spritzer
Fruit Salad
Crab Meat Quiche (p. 62)
Marinated Asparagus
Chocolate Mousse
Iced Tea   Coffee

—LUNCHEON FOR A HOT SUMMER'S DAY—

Frozen Daiquiris
Alligator Pears and Creek Shrimp Salad (p. 47)
Assorted Breads and Rolls   Butter Curls
Fresh Strawberries or Peaches and Cream
Chilled Wines   Iced Coffee

SUPPERS FOR A COLD WINTER'S EVENING

—I—

Tossed Salad
Catch-of-the-Day Bouillabaise (p. 18)
or
Tidalholm Seafood Chowder (p. 24)
or
She-Crab Soup (p. 23, 93)
Corn Sticks or Crackers   Butter
White Wine   Hot Tea

—II—

Piping Hot Fish Stew (p. 20)
Fluffy Rice (optional)   Carrot and Celery Sticks
Sweet Cornbread Muffins   Butter
Hot Tea   Coffee

—III—

Cole Slaw (p. 84)
Fried Fish (p. 35) or Fried Shrimp (p. 39)
Sliced Country Ham   Red Rice
Biscuits   Butter
Hot Apple Pie
Coffee   Tea

CAROLINA CROWD PLEASERS

—ANYTIME—

Green Bean Salad
Frogmore Goulash (p. 44)
Pineapple Fritters
Lemonade   Beer

—SPRING—

Your Catch-of-the-Day Fish (pp. 30-36)
Fresh Asparagus Spears or Dill Salad (p. 84)
Wild Rice Amandine or Scalloped Potatoes
Hot Rolls   Butter
Iced Tea   Beer or White Wine

—FALL—

Cole Slaw (p. 84)
Steamed Shrimp (p. 38), Crabs (p. 57), Oysters (p. 70)
or
Roasted Oysters (p. 70)
Corn-on-the Cob   Butter
Hush Puppies (p. 82) or Garlic Bread
Hot Tea   Beer

BUFFET DINNERS FOR 6-8 PEOPLE

—POT POURRI—

Mixed Green Salad
Island Shrimp Curry (p. 51) in a Rice Ring
Curry Condiments: chopped peanuts, raisins, chutney, flaked (frozen) coconut, bacon bits, etc.
Hot French Bread   Butter
Key Lime Pie
White Wine   Hot Tea

—ORIENTAL—

Saviche (p. 6)
Egg Drop Soup
Shrimp and Chinese Vegetables (p. 43, recipe doubled)
Fluffy Rice   Chow Mein Noodles
Almond Cookies
Hot Green Tea

—SPANISH—

Gazpacho or Chilled Raw Vegetables
Lowcountry Paella (p. 53)
or
Shrimp Creole with Cheese Rice (p. 49)
Hard Rolls   Butter
Flan (Spanish Custard) or Fresh Fruit
Sangria   Coffee

CANDLELIGHT DINNERS

—SURF AND TURF—

Pickled Shrimp (p. 7)
Broiled Tenderloin
Crab Stuffed Potatoes (p. 59)   Broccoli Hollandaise
Sherbet and Cookies
Assorted Wines   Coffee

—FRENCH—

French Onion Soup with Crusty Bread and Cheese
Fresh Spinach with Bacon Bits and Egg Slices
Margaret's Crab Meat Crépes (p. 63)
or
Seafood Omelets (p. 62)
Croissants   Butter
Pot de Créme
White Wine   Café

French Huguenots attempted to settle in Beaufort, S.C. as early at 1562.

CANDLELIGHT DINNERS

—CONTINENTAL—

Trout Amandine (p. 31)
Buttered New Potatoes and Chives and Grated Cheese
Green Beans with Fresh Dill
Assorted Cheeses and Fresh Fruits
White Wine   Coffee

—SOUTHERN—

Lettuce Wedge with Thousand Island Dressing
Made Dish of Shrimp and Crab (p. 40)
Broiled Tomatoes with Basil and Parmesan
Hot Biscuits   Butter   Peach Preserves
Lemon Tarts
White Wine   Coffee

Southern Seafood Secrets are actually the best recipes and hints passed down from many generations occupying the South Carolina Lowcountry. Since 1520, the Spanish, French, English, Scottish, South Carolina, Confederate and United States flags have honored our precious land.

The Name You'll Want To Remember.

The Flavor You'll Never Forget!

Harris Atlantic She-Crab Soup is a most unique and delicious soup. It's rich and zesty with a creamy sauce full of flavorful Atlantic Crabmeat. She-Crab Soup is both lively and delicate with the natural flavor of crab roe in a special Blue Channel recipe. It's perfect for the whole family anytime and for special occasions as well. Harris Atlantic She-Crab Soup is the only soup of its kind in the world. It's the name you'll want to remember. With the flavor you'll never forget.

The Delicate Soups for Hearty Appetites

Harris Atlantic She-Crab Soup
Blue Channel Oyster Stew
Blue Channel Clam Chowder

From the Packers of Harris Atlantic and Blue Channel Crabmeat

Sweetest, most delicate crab meat you can eat comes from the Atlantic Blue Crab and HARRIS packs only the best of it!

$1.00 REFUND OFFER

Send 10 6½ oz. Harris Crab Meat labels along with your name and address to: Blue Channel Company, Refund Offer, Box 128, Port Royal, SC 29935. Blue Channel will send you $1.00 and a full-color **Carolina Crabmeat Recipe** booklet. THIS OFFER EXPIRES DECEMBER 31, 1981.